FENG SHUI

Nicola Jenkins

p

This a Parragon Publishing Book
This edition published in 2002

Parragon Publishing
Queen Street House,
4 Queen Street
Bath BA1 1HE
United Kingdom

This book was created by
THE BRIDGEWATER BOOK COMPANY

A CIP catalogue record for this book is
available from the British Library

ISBN 0-75258-859-1

Printed in China

contents

introduction

The modern practice of Feng Shui is based upon ancient Chinese philosophy. We can use it to bring luck and harmony to our homes and also to our lives.

Life change

If you feel that life is passing you by or that good things only happen to other people, that your relationships or career are a series of disasters, that life itself is far more

HOME MAKEOVER *Feng Shui can be incorporated into your personal taste and plans for your home—it will help you to give each room just the right feel.*

frustrating than it should be, and you want to do something to fix it—then it's time to cast aside any reservations and look at how Feng Shui can be used to even the score. This ancient art of placement is based on the idea that your relationship with your environment affects every other aspect of your life; rearrange your home, office, or yard to encourage a more auspicious flow of energy, and you'll notice immediate improvements.

Universal planning

Feng Shui is used by people all over the world to ensure that their homes and workplaces fulfill the special laws for

MONEY CHARM *This three-legged frog is used in Feng Shui to bring wealth and prosperity.*

auspicious arrangement. These laws can be applied to on any scale—whether it's planning the position of a city, placing a house, or moving a table in your living room. Today Feng Shui is mostly used to help position and layout homes and offices, but you can use it on whatever level of design or positioning you wish.

HAPPY HOMES *Feng Shui can be used to enhance your home and improve the fortunes of each member of the family.*

feng shui today

Although the tradition of Feng Shui dates back thousands of years, it has experienced a surge of interest in recent years. It has been updated and modified to apply it to the way we live today.

Long ago...

Feng Shui was first developed in China some 4000–7000 years ago, although the ideas governing this fascinating subject are similar to those found in other parts of the world. The fundamental concept at the heart of Feng Shui is the desire for balance, unity, and harmony in every aspect of the home and of life. When you have a harmonious relationship with your

DRAGON GUARD *Dragons fill Chinese mythology. In Feng Shui, they are one of the four guardian animals who protect sites from bad fortune.*

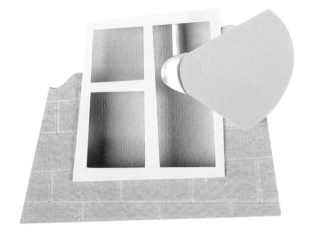

HOME GUARD *If you live in an apartment block, use a bright light in your window to fend off oppressive energy from any large, overlooking buildings.*

environment—in terms of where your home is situated, the buildings or landscape around it, and the placement of each object within your home—then all other aspects of your life begin to flow more easily. On this basic tenet all the other rules of Feng Shui are founded.

New for old

Translating the ancient principles of Feng Shui for use in the modern world has not changed any of its fundamentals. Feng Shui practitioners still analyze the flow of energy around the home and work out the effect of improved arrangement.

GOOD TURTLE *This venerable creature is one of the animal guardians in Feng Shui.*

MONEY MAKER *The practice of Feng Shui is believed to be able to bring wealth and prosperity to the user.*

MONEY LUCK *Red is an auspicious color for business—and coins tied with red ribbon are used in Feng Shui to help encourage prosperity.*

7

feng shui today

The Feng Shui tradition is ancient and complex. Modern practitioners have come up with several different methods for using the wisdom of the ancients. This book focuses on one of the easiest schools to study.

Feng Shui schools

There are several different styles of Feng Shui prevalent in the West. All strive toward the same ideal—of balance in all things—and there is a certain amount of overlap of ideas. The main difference lies in the approach. Compass Method uses a luo pan to detect energy blockages throughout the building, and also relies on additional information about the occupants in order to work out the most auspicious areas of the house for

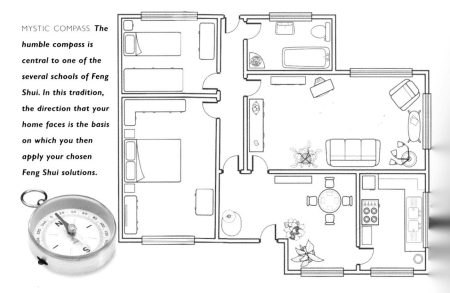

MYSTIC COMPASS *The humble compass is central to one of the several schools of Feng Shui. In this tradition, the direction that your home faces is the basis on which you then apply your chosen Feng Shui solutions.*

them to sleep, work, and play in. Eight House takes a reading from the front of the house, using a modern compass, to work out which of the eight segments of the house is best for the occupants (see The Eight Directions, page 22). Form School emphasizes the importance of the surrounding landscape as a means of explaining any disharmonies arising.

The Pa kua

Black Hat Sect, sometimes referred to as intuitive Feng Shui, is the easiest to work with for those who are just beginning to use Feng Shui as it starts from your front door, and from each doorway you enter thereafter. It uses the pa kua (see page 26) to identify energy blockages, and is the method this book will focus on.

What follows is a brief look at the range of ideas you can use to identify the areas in your home or surroundings that may be adversely affecting your health, finances, creativity, relationships, and much more. Take these ideas, add your own willingness to make changes, clear your clutter, place a cure, and wait for results.

PA KUA SQUARES *The pa kua helps Feng Shui analysis of an area by splitting the space up into distinct zones that refer to different areas of life.*

Fortunate Blessings	Fame	Relationships
The Elders	Unity/Tao	Children/ Creativity
Contemplation	The Journey/ Career	Helpful Friends/ Travel

'If it isn't broken, don't fix it!'

It is worth working out exactly which areas of your life you wish to enhance before applying Feng Shui. Avoid changing areas that you are happy with.

Life repairs

The most important thing to remember as you start to work with the principles of Feng Shui is not to get overenthusiastic and place cures in every area of your house. The cures work—so don't alter anything unless you want to change that aspect of your life. This is especially important to bear in mind if you are generally happy with how things are going, but would just like to adjust a couple of individual issues. In this case, concentrate on the areas where you do want to make changes and start small— little cures are just as effective.

Remember, balance in all things! If you really want to change something, that doesn't mean you need to overload the related areas of your home with cures.

WEALTH BOWL *Give your finances a boost with a wealth bowl. This is a bowl filled with items which represent wealth and prosperity to you.*

Let's take relationships as an example. Say you have been happily single for quite some time, then one day something happens to make you change your mind. You want a relationship yesterday, thank you! Too many cures packed into the relationship area could end up in adverse effects occurring—you might be sending out the "desperate" message which could bring you nothing (especially if you don't take into account the Five Elements, see page 18). Far worse, you might attract a life situation that is wholly inappropriate for you, bringing further chaos. The properly placed cure helps to improve the flow of energy into and out of your life, encouraging what is beneficial toward you, and possibly speeding up the arrival of your would-be lover.

CLEAN ENERGY **There are plenty of subtle but effective energy cleansing techniques you can use—such as using an incense stick.**

BAD LUCK **A dead or unhealthy plant will bring bad luck to your office or workplace.**

LOVE MATCH **You can also use Feng Shui to increase your chances of finding romance.**

11

chi energy

Chi is the essential energy that flows through everything in the universe, creating life. Behaving like wind, water, or electricity, Chi can be directed and channeled.

Life force

The word "Chi" refers to the life-giving energy that flows into, out of, and around everything in the universe.

Chi is vital to life, and the study of the flow of Chi energy (as well as what alters it) is the basis not only of Feng Shui, but also of the study of ley lines, the chakras, acupuncture, acupressure, kinesiology, and many other traditions.

We become aware of Chi and its subtle changes, for example, when we walk into a "charged atmosphere" where people have been fighting, or when we are aware of the moods or energy levels of a place.

INNER CHI **Practices such as meditation help us to get in tune with the Chi that flows through our bodies as well as our lives.**

The various schools of Feng Shui show you how to orient yourself and the movable parts of your environment so that you are in alignment with the flow of energy, making it easier for you to attain your goals and to live in harmony with your surroundings. Feng Shui aims to encourage Chi to flow gently and beneficially through the home.

GENTLE CHI *The most beneficial floor plans let Chi flow easily to all areas of the home. In this example, Chi can enter the space and reach all of the rooms easily. There are no long corridors that might channel the energy to travel with too much force and therefore be damaging.*

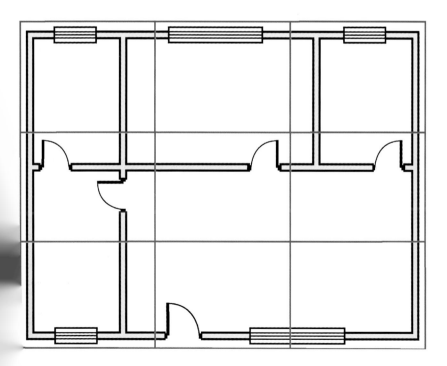

the principles of feng shui

One of the fundamental concepts of Feng Shui is that of Yin and Yang. These ever-opposing energies combine to create harmony in the universe and in our lives.

Yin and Yang

Chi flows along a continuum between Yin (passive energy) and Yang (active energy). Everything can therefore be described as either more Yin or more Yang, depending on what it is compared with. All things are a mixture of Yin and Yang energy in various degrees of balance and harmony.

Everything seeks to balance the flow of energy between itself and its environment, so minute adjustments in the balance between Yin and Yang are constantly occurring naturally, to keep things stable.

LAND SIGNS *Landscapes have Yin and Yang elements—mountains and deserts are yang, rivers and greenery are yin.*

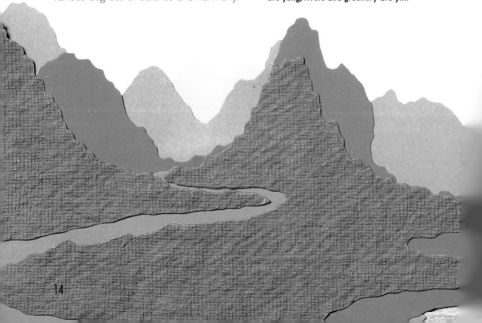

Feng Shui tool

You can use the concept of Yin and Yang to alter the flow of Chi in your home, office, or yard. The easiest way of doing this is by changing the shapes, colors, textures, or artwork that surround you. The larger the area altered, or the more prominent the artwork, the stronger the overall effect on your home and life.

As you become more familiar with Feng Shui you will begin to be able to tell instinctively whether an object, building, or room is strong in Yin or Yang energy, or whether it is well-balanced.

ETERNAL HARMONY *Passive Yin and active Yang cannot exist without each other and are in eternal balance.*

the principles of feng shui

There are times when the flow of Chi adversely affects your health and general welfare. Awareness of the problem and the use of simple remedies can bring about immediate and effective results.

Chi Lessons

Look out for the following signs of harmful Chi. *Cutting Chi*—when energy flows past a sharp corner it can affect the current and direction of flow or start it moving off at an angle. Being hit by Cutting Chi can lead

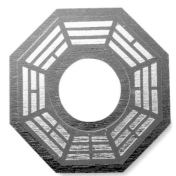

PA KUA MIRROR **The pa kua mirror is a powerful tool for reflecting harmful Chi, and is useful for entrances and windows.**

to ill health. Block the effects of Cutting Chi outside your home by dense planting or by reflecting it back using shiny door fixtures or pa kua mirrors. Cutting Chi inside the house can be softened using plants or adding tablecloths. Look for furniture with rounded edges.

NATURAL CHI **Plants are a source of healthy Chi. Choose broad-leaf plants rather than spiky ones such as cacti.**

Keep on moving

Stagnant Chi—when Chi moves too slowly, you may find that you are feeling stuck in a rut, that your life is moving slowly, that you feel unmotivated or depressed, or experience some health problems. Stagnant Chi is emphasized where there is clutter, little natural light, or dark corners. To address the problem, clear up the room, air it regularly, add lights to dark corners or tall spiky plants—this is a good use for the Yucca, not normally a plant used for Feng Shui cures.

Speedy Chi

Chi moving too fast—when Chi moves too fast through your home, you may feel that luck or life passes you by, that you feel insecure, paranoid, or that you are working too fast for your comfort. Begin to slow things down by introducing some of the Feng Shui window treatments in your home, or by placing cures in front of the window (as shown). Wind chimes or Earth-related cures seem to be the most effective solution in this situation.

The negative effects of additional pressure from overhead structures, such as beams, can also be reduced using cures that "lift" the energy of the room, for instance light and airy window arrangements, tall plants, uplighters, or musical instruments.

CRYSTAL FILTERS **Crystals placed near windows will help to absorb any harmful energy trying to enter from outside.**

CHERRY OPAL

AMETHYST

BLUE LACE AGATE

JADE

five elements

The five elements trace the journey of Chi through nature. We can use them to bring auspicious qualities into our homes. They also serve to balance the overall flow of Chi through the home.

Energy flow

The Five Elements—Earth, Water, Fire, Wood, and Metal—are used to describe the changing qualities of Chi. If you compare Chi to the seasons, you would start at the height of spring (Wood) as nature begins to awaken. We then move into the heat of summer (Fire). The Fall harvest is represented by Earth. Winter comes bringing with it the inward-moving Chi of Metal. As winter dissipates, you get the rainfall (Water) needed for life, and the cycle begins again.

ELEMENTAL **The five elements, central to the practice of Feng Shui, move in two transformational cycles of energy.**

PRODUCTIVE CYCLE
Each element creates the next in the cycle.

DESTRUCTIVE CYCLE
Each element destroys the next in the cycle.

The Five Elements work closely together to support each other and to achieve balance between them. If one element is weak or deficient, the Chi of the element that would normally support it moves into the destructive cycle and "attacks" the element that usually drains it. For instance, Water normally supports Wood. If Wood is weak, Water flows toward Fire and puts it out. The destructive cycle can be used to create positive effects, for instance if there is an excessive amount of one particular element in the room. However, you can get more positive effects by enhancing the element that is weak.

WATER WORKS *Decorative items depicting one of the elements can be used to enhance that element's qualities.*

FAKE FIRE *Red objects can be used to evoke the qualities of Fire, and plants are a good source of the Wood element.*

five elements theory

Each of the five elements (Earth, Water, Fire, Wood, and Metal) represents a unique form of Chi energy. They are used in Feng Shui for the specific effects they have on fortune and prosperity.

Elements of design

Use the Five Elements to enhance an area (by adding a cure which represents the element that feeds it—say Wood if the area relates to Fire), to maintain an area (add more of that same element—Fire in this case), or to correct it where it is overemphasized (add the element that drains it—Earth drains Fire). Five Element theory becomes vitally important when you are trying to consider what aspects you want to bring to a particular area. If things are moving too slowly or you want more passion in your life, add Fire. When things are moving too fast or you're feeling insecure, add Earth cures. Additional growth or vitality in a particular area requires a Wood cure.

FORMS OF ENERGY **The five elements each represent Chi in a different form. Chi flows between them in endless cycles of creation and destruction.**

Metal is great if you are looking to organize yourself or enrich your holdings. Water, meanwhile, is essential if you want to add depth to relationships, more flexibility into your life, and more tranquillity and peacefulness in general.

Indoor elements

Wood energy can be represented by tall plants, wooden and paper objects, vertical stripes, all artwork to do with plants, and all shades of the color green.

Consider Fire in the placement of stoves, fireplaces, lighting, triangular objects, candles, or anything pointed or serrated in shape. Look for the color red if you really want to inject some fire into your life!

Terracotta pots, china, clay, or plaster objects represent Earth, as do all objects that are longer than they are tall, natural fibers, and all shades of yellow and brown.

Any metallic object carries Metal energy, as do white, gold and silver, and all round, domed, or circular-shaped objects.

To add Water energy to an area, look at using glass, mirrors, irregular or wavy shapes, the color black, trailing plants, or indoor water features.

ELEMENTS OF DESIGN *The five elements can easily be incorporated into the home using decorative objects such as plants, pictures, ornaments, and vases.*

the eight directions

The eight compass directions are used in a number of Feng Shui schools. Each direction has associations and is linked with one of the Lo Shu magic square numbers.

Find the way

These refer to compass headings taken from the center of your home, using a modern compass, and are essential reference points for one of the popular approaches to Feng Shui. If you compare the attributes listed here with those found in the pa kua (see page 26), you will note

HEALTH POINTS *Each of the compass points has associations with elements and different aspects of life.*

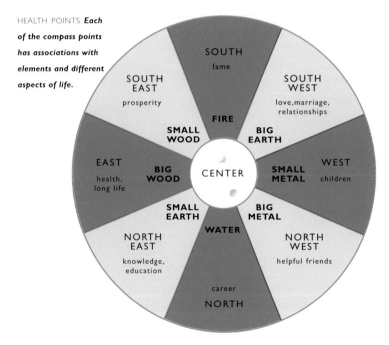

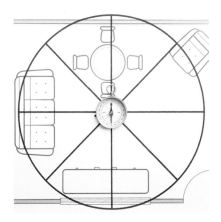

LUCK FINDER *The compass method matches areas of the home with specific areas of life and one of the elements.*

EASY FENG SHUI *The Eight Directions method can be used as an alternative to the pa kua method.*

LUCK ZONES *We can divide a room into the various zones of the Lo Shu square to work out which areas need attention.*

that there is quite a lot of common material. This is provided for your information, particularly for those who may find that despite general good luck and happiness in their lives, their home bears no resemblance whatsoever to the intuitive layout provided by the pa kua. If this is the case, get out your compass: you may have unconsciously aligned yourself in the traditional way; in which case this method will be more appropriate for your continuing good fortunes.

the five celestial animals

The five celestial animals are represented in the landscape surrounding
a site. If you live in a city, they are reflected in neighboring buildings.
Ideal sites have all of the animals represented around them.

Watch dogs

The five mythical beasts used in Feng Shui
(the Turtle, the Dragon, the Tiger, the
Phoenix, and the Snake) are present in the
surroundings of any home and in any
landscape. They can be used to explain
how the landscape surrounding your
home can have an effect on your health as
well as explaining the most psychologically
comfortable environment to live in—one
in which your surroundings cradle you as if
in an armchair, with solid support to the
rear (turtle), a good view in front
(phoenix), and balance to either side. An
overbearing tiger, for instance, may leave
you feeling under attack from neighbors or
even from family members.

Well placed

Feng Shui masters look for sites in which
all the celestial animals are represented in
the surrounding environment. In the
countryside this will relate to hills and
mountains. For example, a small hill in

BEASTLY LANDSCAPE *A highly auspicious
setting for a home has a line of Dragon
hills running down the left side and Tiger
hills running down the right. The Dragon
hills are the more important of the two.*

LUCKY SYMBOLS *The good luck associated with four animals can be found in objects depicting them.*

front of the home is very auspicious as it represents the presence of the Phoenix. A range of hills, preferably behind the site, represents the Turtle. Large Dragon hills should lie on the left of the house and smaller Tigers to the right.

PERFECT PLACE *An ideal setting—with the celestial or guardian animals represented in the surrounding hills. Such a house is likely to bring good fortune and happiness to its inhabitants.*

the pa kua

The pa kua is a highly practical Feng Shui tool that allows the user to "read" the flow of Chi in all areas of the home and the rooms within it. Once the reading has been completed, improvements can be made.

What it is and how to use it

The pa kua developed out of extensive study of the *I Ching*, or *Book of Changes*. It provides you with a Feng Shui map, suggesting the most comfortable way you can align your life with the flow of Chi in your environment. Each of the outer eight squares of the pa kua is represented by one of the trigrams used in the *I Ching*. These trigrams, individually and together, encompass every possible spiritual, mental, physical, and emotional change that can occur in your life. When each sector of the home is in harmony as specified by the pa kua, the whole place is in balance. This is why we find the symbol for unity and balance at the center of the pa kua.

Pa kua system

With intuitive Feng Shui, you always align the pa kua with the doorway you have entered, as shown. You also start a new

YIN YANG SYMBOLS *The trigrams are made up of three lines—broken lines represent Yin, continuous lines Yang.*

alignment each time you enter a new area of the room, where it has been visually cordoned off in some way.

As you work in this way, you will note that each time you move into a new room, the pa kua is rotating slightly. This means that cures placed in certain areas will be particularly powerful. Imagine that your house is in layers, just like an onion. You start at the front door with a floor plan for the entire house. As you move on to the rooms where you spend the most time and then to particular areas of those rooms, so the importance of those areas to your overall well-being increases.

Consider the Fortunate Blessings corners, for instance. If you are storing unpaid bills, trash, or dirty clothes in these areas, things are likely to be less than satisfactory.

THE BAGUA *Feng shui practitioners work by laying a pa kua template over the plan of the area they are analyzing.*

S

SE			SW
WIND *Fortunate Blessings*	**fire** ILLUMINATION *Fame*	*Relationships*	
wood THUNDER *The Elders*	**earth** *Unity/Tao*	**metal** THE LAKE *Children/ Creativity*	
MOUNTAIN *Knowledge and Contemplation*	**water** *The Journey/ Career*	HEAVEN *Helpful Friends/ Travel*	
NE			NW

E   W

N

◄——— DOORWAY ALONG BOTTOM SECTION OF PA KUA ———►

missing pa kua areas— and how to fix them

The pa kua template might not match the shape of your room exactly. In this situation there are some specific solutions that you can use to enhance the missing areas—without rebuilding your home!

Pa kua additions

The pa kua can be used for any shape of home or room as long as it remains proportionally the same. When you have extensions or missing areas (as shown)

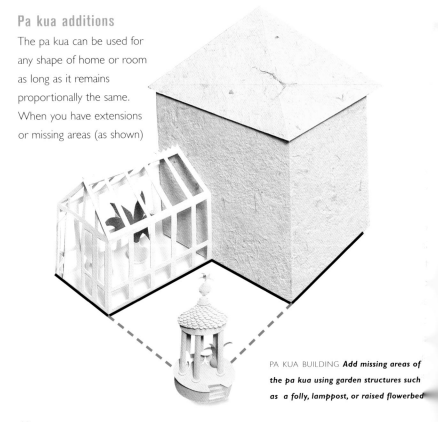

PA KUA BUILDING **Add missing areas of the pa kua using garden structures such as a folly, lamppost, or raised flowerbed**

LIGHT THE WAY *One method for replacing a missing area and enjoying its associated luck is to illuminate the corresponding area of the yard.*

missing section. If you do not have a yard, the appropriate cures include using large mirrors in the areas next to the missing section in order to suggest expansion and provide an illusion of completion. Five Element cures (see page 18) are also important here in order to enhance the missing elements that you would have had, were the pa kua represented completely.

you need to consider how happy you are with the aspect of your life "missing" from the pa kua. If you are not satisfied, consider placing cures to include the missing area and concentrate on the other areas of your home which relate to that issue.

If your home includes a yard, you can look at ways of building something in the yard to make a visual link between the missing space and your home. If circumstances allow it, you might consider an extension or a conservatory. Other options that are also more than satisfactory include placing an outside lamp, a large water feature, raised planting beds with large colorful plants or a tree at the point that marks the corner of the

MISSING LINKS *Yard structures can be used to stand in for missing pa kua areas in the home. A pond is a good choice as it is a beneficial addition in its own right, especially with fish added to it.*

what if your toilet is in the wrong place?

Toilets can be viewed with suspicion in Feng Shui. They could be literally flushing good Chi out of the home altogether. Luckily, there are a number of steps that you can take to counter the bad effect they have.

Unlucky bathrooms

The best place for the bathroom is in the Wood section of the pa kua, as Water feeds Wood in the Five Elements cycle. This is also why it is advantageous to add a few tall or bushy plants to the area if you are wanting to soak up some of that watery energy. However, some things just cannot be moved. If your toilet does happen to be in the Fortunate Blessings, Career, or Relationship areas of your home (for instance), look at ways of

BALANCING ACT *Add Wood using a mirror with a wooden frame or a plant to balance your toilet.*

DEALING WITH TOILET TROUBLE

As toilets are unlucky however carefully they are situated in the home, Feng Shui recommends a number of simple, practical suggestions that can be taken to counteract the bad energy that they create, and also stop them flushing away all the good energy from your home and your life. Try some of these simple steps:

- Keep the toilet seat closed
- Keep the bathroom door closed
- When choosing a toilet, select one that is small and inconspicuous.
- Enhance the corresponding pa kua areas in other rooms of the house.

FIRE POWER *Candles, especially those made with red wax, will add the Fire element and help to balance the Water represented in the bathroom—in particular by toilets. Always take care when placing candles anywhere in the home.*

adjusting the appearance of the bathroom in order to prevent Chi from being flushed away. This could involve finding ways to reduce the watery element in an area where you might want a little more Fire. Why not add plants, plus red towels or candles to the room?

Other very simple cures include keeping the lid down when not in use, airing the room regularly, and adding the elements you want to enhance. If you have the opportunity to plan the layout of your home, try to give the toilet as auspicious placement as possible. Avoid placing it in areas relating to crucial areas of your life.

UNLUCKY TOILET *There is a range of steps that you can take to counteract the Chi-draining effects of toilets.*

31

clearing clutter

You can introduce all the cures that you like, but if your home remains cluttered, then it is unlikely that the cures will work. They could even have negative effects.

Life blockage

Clearing clutter is the most important thing you can do when you start to work with Feng Shui. It cannot be overlooked if you want your cures to work. Getting rid of clutter (or organizing it) can help to unblock stagnant Chi and, if you are ruthless with your cleaning, can sometimes effect the desired change before you have a chance to place your cure. Simply placing a cure in an area that is cluttered will either prevent it from working or (especially with mirrors and crystals) will actually increase the problem instead of fixing it. Clear the clutter first.

Clutter takes many forms. As well as the detritus of modern living, it can include everything you have been holding on to—outmoded clothing, furniture, ideas, photographs, or emotions. It can also include what is sometimes referred to as Predecessor Energy—the emotional energy left behind by the people who previously lived in your home. It can be a good idea to find out the circumstances o⁻

GOOD ENERGY *Homes that are free from clutter will greatly improve the flow of Chi and allow room for lucky events.*

the former tenants—if you find that they had similar problems to those you are currently facing, it is time for a thorough spring cleaning, to look seriously at the issues raised, find appropriate cures, and—before placing them—do a space-clearing exercise.

Space clearing can be done in a number of different ways. One of the easiest

methods involves using soundmakers, such as a bell, and walking around each room in the house chiming the bell at intervals. Another method involves using a couple of drops of essential oils—such as juniper, frankincense, or lemon—mixed with water in a spray mister, then spraying it throughout each room in the house. If you are not satisfied with your own space clearing, there are professionals specializing in space clearing or, alternatively, contact a qualified Reiki practitioner.

CLEAR THE AIR *A wind chime can serve to energize Chi and so clear away residual negative energy.*

SIMPLE DECOR *A few simple decorative items will have much greater impact in straightforward design terms than a mass of cluttering objects. This also makes for good Feng Shui.*

BAD, OLD ENERGY

The previous occupants of your home may have left some of their energy behind. This can interfere with your harmony. Use a small bell to go around your home and clear this old energy. This is most effective if it follows a session of uncluttering and cleaning.

general cures

Anything can be used as a Feng Shui cure, and some of the most popular items are illustrated on the next few pages. The most important aspect of choosing a cure is that you really have to like it.

Feng Shui improvements

Colors are useful cures and can be used to represent the Five Elements. Any shade or hue will do, so pick the ones that you feel happiest with. The larger the area of color, the more effect it has on your life.

Mirrors help to activate Chi and Water energy. For best effects, they need to be absolutely spotless, undamaged, and reflect something pleasant. Mirrors are best avoided in the bedroom as they disturb sleep, especially if the sleeper can see their reflection while lying in bed.

Lighting can be used to bring Fire energy into missing areas or to lighten up corners that might collect stagnant Chi. Any form of lighting will do, although

TROUBLE SPOTS **As well as adding cures, look for problem areas, such as beam lying directl over beds**

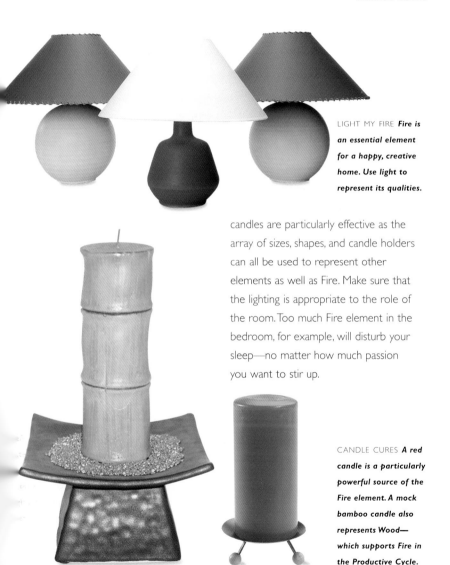

LIGHT MY FIRE *Fire is an essential element for a happy, creative home. Use light to represent its qualities.*

candles are particularly effective as the array of sizes, shapes, and candle holders can all be used to represent other elements as well as Fire. Make sure that the lighting is appropriate to the role of the room. Too much Fire element in the bedroom, for example, will disturb your sleep—no matter how much passion you want to stir up.

CANDLE CURES *A red candle is a particularly powerful source of the Fire element. A mock bamboo candle also represents Wood— which supports Fire in the Productive Cycle.*

general cures

There is a wide variety of ways to introduce Feng Shui cures to your home—enough to suit most tastes and styles. Try some of the following ideas.

Crystal clear

Crystals serve to activate energy, particularly Water energy. The majority of uses for crystals in Feng Shui focus on the small, multifaceted lead crystals which can be hung in windows or unobtrusive places to great effect. Natural crystals are also popular cures, especially as each variety is associated with specific properties. If you use natural crystals, pick ones that have smooth surfaces and that feel comfortable to you when you hold them—this increases their effect.

ENERGY BOOST *Wind chimes help to enliven Chi and keep it circulating*

Soundmakers, such as wind chimes, bells, clocks, or musical instruments help to attract good luck and can lift the atmosphere of a room, or slow the flow of Chi where it is too fast moving. For them to be effective, you must enjoy the sound that they make.

Living things of any description also activate Chi. Healthy plants and flowers activate Wood, while pets and wildlife bring in the Fire element. For best effect, plants need to be soft and round-leaf as well as regularly fed and watered.

AMETHYST

ROSE QUARTZ

CLEAR QUARTZ

Unhealthy plants need to be nurtured back to life or disposed of before they affect the health of the home.

Potpourri and dried flowers are not advisable additions to your home as they represent death, decay, and desiccation. Check for dried plants in your Fortunate Blessings or Career areas. If you absolutely have to have them, then look at placing them where they can't adversely affect you—possibly next to a large, extremely healthy plant. If you do want something representing Wood in an area where plants are unable to grow—

say where there is minimal light—then silk or artificial plants are more effective.

Natural objects such as rocks, shells, incense, and essential oils help to refresh Earth energy and are useful if you want to stabilize certain areas of your life.

Water features of all kinds, from indoor water fountains down to bowls of water or essential oil vaporizers, help to stimulate Water energy and refresh Chi. These are especially good in the Career and Fortunate Blessings sectors of the home. An aquarium is a great combination of water, movement, and life.

INDOOR FLOW **Water features bring the Water element into the home.**

SCENT CURE **Oil burners will add the scent of essential oils to a room.**

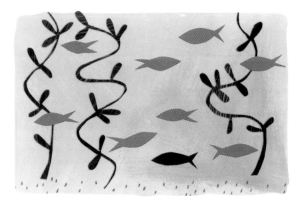

how to install a cure

Cures can take a few weeks to work and sometimes things get worse before they get better. Have patience and try a variety of cures for different effects.

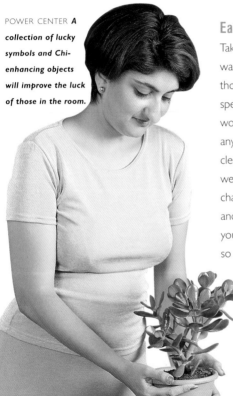

POWER CENTER *A collection of lucky symbols and Chi-enhancing objects will improve the luck of those in the room.*

Easy does it

Take things slowly; identify the area you want to work with—focusing initially on those rooms in your home where you spend the most time—then having worked out what cure to use and cleared any clutter first, place your cure, visualizing clearly what you want it to do. Wait six weeks, and if you haven't seen a positive change in that time, then revisit the issue, and look for other clues. It may be that you are sending out conflicting messages—so you might want to see what you are "saying" in the other parts of the house that relate to that issue in your life. Nor does it mean that you necessarily have to change the location of your front door. Feng Shui allows you to work with what you've got and make corrections where you need to encourage things to flow more readily. Be patient before looking for alternatives if a cure doesn't seem to work at first.

When does a cure start to work?

You can expect your Feng Shui cure to produce results in under six weeks—and often much faster than that. If you are pleased with the way it is working, remember that the most effective way of increasing your fortunes in this area is to look after the cures you have placed, watering plants regularly, changing dead flower arrangements, dusting paintings,

CHI CHIME *A wind chime will enliven Chi in the home with its tinkling sound. Use it to keep Chi moving through areas where it might otherwise grow stagnant, and at windows and doors.*

CRYSTAL BATH *Restore the effect of crystals by soaking them in salt water overnight. This will clear out any negative energy that they have absorbed.*

mirrors, and crystals, and so on. This is one of the reasons that a regular spring cleaning is good for you and your home. Maintain your cures and they will carry on working at their full capacity.

39

focusing on...

The Elders/Authority: Health and Family. This area of the pa kua affects your relationships with figures of authority, your health, and your energy levels.

Storm warning

The trigram for this area of the pa kua relates to Thunder—the natural warning of storms on the horizon and the potential for a profound display of power. Storms can herald devastating change and can serve as a reminder that you are smaller and less powerful than they are; that survival involves having a strong constitution, plenty of support from those closest to you, and the will to persevere. There are positive aspects also: from sudden change spring plenty of opportunities for growth, hence the Wood element springs from here, and we also associate this area with all the people who

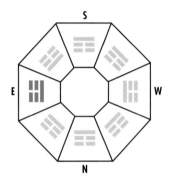

HEALTH CHARMS *Both the tortoise and the crane are symbols of longevity and bring health and good luck.*

represent respected authority and who rein our lives—parents, teachers, and employers of all descriptions.

This is the area that needs looking at if you are experiencing difficulties relating to any authority figure, with relatives, or with those on whom you rely for support (outside of any one-to-one relations). It is also useful to place a cure in this area if you have been suffering from ill health, a lack of motivation, or loss of energy.

Effective cures to use in this area include everything that represents the Wood element, but especially tall, healthy plants and fresh flowers. If you choose to use artwork or photos here, pick landscapes showing tranquil, bright, sunny scenes, and avoid any that hint at bad weather brewing. Blue and green items, floral prints, and anything you associate positively with health will also enhance the Chi in this area.

TRANQUIL IMAGES **Photographs or paintings of calm, restful scenes will enhance the strength of this area of the pa kua. Avoid stormy, moody pictures.**

focusing on...

Fortunate Blessings: Wealth and Prosperity. This section of the pa kua relates to the money and business aspects of your life. It will also help to bring calm and peace into your life and remove stress and worry.

Winds of wealth

The home of Wind energy, the Fortunate Blessings sector is the area to focus on if you need to improve your financial situation, if you are currently unlucky in your business affairs or career, or if you wish to be more aware of both abundance and luck as they flow through your home and your life. It is also works on comfort and enjoying life.

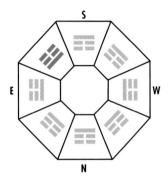

The wind does not flow fast and furiously through this sector (normally). Imagine instead that it is a gentle, warm breeze which can take the chill off your life and make things more comfortable. Cures in this area will help you improve your situation slowly and healthily, as long as you are patient for the results and persistent in your efforts.

GOLDEN CHARM *Golden objects are a universal symbol of wealth and are an effective cure in this area of the pa kua. Don't overload this area.*

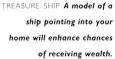

TREASURE SHIP *A model of a ship pointing into your home will enhance chances of receiving wealth.*

MONEY CHARM *Coins tied together with lucky red ribbon will enhance your money-making skills and increase prosperity.*

Do not sit back and expect the cure to do all the work. The right cure will encourage opportunities for success into your life, but you need to take advantage of them when they arrive. Appropriate

MONEY PLANT *This species of plant with round leaves is a potent cure to place in this area. Keep it free from dust and healthy.*

cures include anything of value, such as antiques, or things that make you feel wealthy and aware of the finer things in life. Rich colors and fabrics in blues, purples, and reds are particularly auspicious here, as are plants with either round leaves (Metal element) or flowers in reds and purples.

This is not a good place to store clutter of any description; dirty clothes, records, or administration will have a negative effect on your financial situation.

focusing on...

Illumination: Fame and Reputation. We all need recognition and the respect of our friends and colleagues. Use this section of the pa kua to improve your self-esteem and help you get on in your career.

Lighting the way

The home of Fire, this section must be carefully treated. In balance it can warm you and all those around you, giving you opportunities to be creative, to enjoy a good reputation, to be highly regarded, and sought-after for the work that you do. It can also have a very exciting effect on your social life. Too much fire, however, can

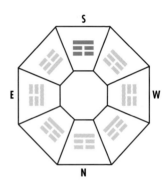

burn your fingers and leave you burning your bridges with others. Your reputation might suffer and you may find yourself kept at arms' length by others, feeling lonely and unappreciated. This section needs enhancing if you are experiencing difficulties in achieving the recognition you desire, problems progressing in your chosen career, if you are suffering from

PROUD PAST **Display certificates or any prizes you have won. These add to the Fire element by boosting your inner energy and self-esteem.**

a debilitating lack of self-confidence, particularly in relation to your work, or if you need help supporting or salvaging your reputation.

Fire at home

Cures that will enhance this area include displaying any academic awards that you have earned or acknowledgments for your work. Artwork relating to animals, people, fire, sunlight, or light in general are also effective here, as are the color red and all things that suggest the shape of a flame (triangular, conical, and pyramid-shaped items). It is best to introduce cures for this area gradually and then be patient for results. Too many cures may lead to too much Fire energy, resulting in distracting and unfocused energy in your life. This could cause you to make bad decisions and lose your temper with friends and family.

LUCKY LUK *This figure represents the Chinese household god Luk. You can use any figure that you respect as a cure in this area.*

DOUBLE EFFECT *The combination of the color red, representing Fire, and the symbol of the horse invites fame, recognition, and respect into your life.*

focusing on...

Relationships: Love and Marriage. Central to most people's happiness is the health of their relationships. Use this section of the pa kua to enhance your love life.

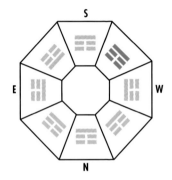

The love zone

This area always attracts a great deal of interest, whether one-to-one relationships exist, are developing, or are currently stormy or stale. This area is the most Yin sector of the pa kua. When it is missing from a floor plan, women in particular tend to miss it and so feel uncomfortable in the home. Use cures to enhance it.

In balance, this sector encourages partners to offer each other unconditional support, trust, and nurturing. Out of balance, there can often be a power struggle in the home or a coldness between the residents.

The first step to a healthy relationship is to love and accept yourself. Cures placed in the relationship area will help to attract relationships where they are missing, or rebalance and enhance existing ones. They will, however, focus initially on helping

HAPPY COUPLES *It is best to use pairs of objects in this area to enhance the theme of relationship and love.*

MARRIAGE MAKER *This crystal bowl filled with water, pebbles, and flowers is used to enhance marriage prospects.*

When your bedroom isn't in the relationship area, you can still work with what is in that area to enhance love and romance as well as looking at the relationship area of your bedroom. Concentrate on making the lighting soft and gentle, not harsh, and try to choose only natural fibers for your bedding.

you improve your relationship with yourself. Effective cures include artwork relating to your significant other or to the features and characteristics you admire or would like in your partner. Other cures tend to be placed in pairs in this area—pairs of candles, plants that have round or soft leaves, flowers in red, pink, or white, pillows, and any symbols you associate with love. It is important to avoid putting solitary items in this area as this can increase any sense of loneliness that is affecting you. The relationship area is also a good place to put all things that are soft or that cradle the body; pillows, comfortable chairs (preferably large enough for two), or beds.

HAPPY SYMBOL *Using objects with the double happiness symbol enhances relationship stability.*

RICH IN LOVE *By introducing crystals into your home you can enhance the health of your love.*

focusing on...

Creativity: Children and Creativity. We can forget that we are all naturally creative. This area enhances the creative child in all of us.

Creative zone

This sector encourages you to look at ways of expressing your inner creativity. This may have become blocked since childhood, so we have to make an effort to recapture the sense of wonder and magic that we had as children, and of simply having fun. It brings to bear all those aspects we associate with a happy child, so it is no surprise that the cures in this area are things that children would like or would create: art supplies, pictures that

DRAGON ENERGY *The dragon symbol brings good luck, and is good for enhancing creativity.*

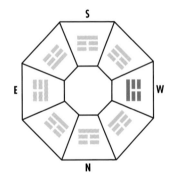

YOUNG ENERGY *Get in touch with your natural creativity with simple activities such as drawing.*

inspire you, and artwork featuring or drawn by children. We all need to be able to let our hair down and have fun every now and again. If you feel that your reserve or inhibitions are holding you back in life, then this is the area to work on. This area is also the home of the Metal element, so all metal items, plus white and pastel colors, are appropriate as cures.

RED BAMBOO **These bamboo tubes with red ribbon enliven Chi and help creative energy to flow in your home.**

UPLIFTING BLOOMS **Bright, fresh flowers enliven Chi and also serve to bring a sense of gaiety into your home. This will in turn help to strengthen your inner child.**

OLD COINS **Ancient Chinese coins can be used as good luck charms in the home and provide the Metal element.**

Life center

This is the area of the pa kua for you to concentrate on if you are trying to get pregnant, you are wanting to experience more creativity in your life, you feel frustrated or unable to work creatively, or you need to improve your existing relationships with your children. If you have been experiencing problems in any of these areas, check to see what "messages" your home is currently giving out about you. Is this where the clutter is stored? Or the dried flowers are displayed? Think carefully about the cures you place.

focusing on...

Helpful Friends and Travel. This Yang section of the pa kua is full of positive energy. It will help to explore new areas of your life, either in work or relationships.

Travel bug

This sector is the most Yang area of the pa kua. Cures placed here will help to enhance your awareness of moving toward your destiny, of increasing

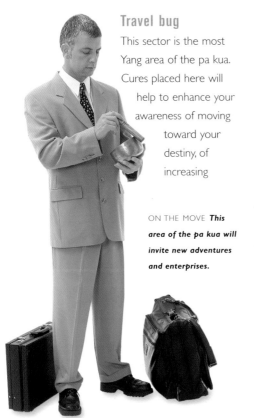

ON THE MOVE *This area of the pa kua will invite new adventures and enterprises.*

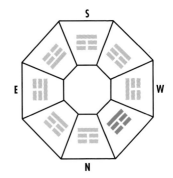

opportunities to be in the right place at the right time, and of attracting toward you more clients, customers, and mentors, the people who help to make your life unfold with ease, inspiration, and loads of fun. This is the area to install cures if you are wanting to do any of these things, or to travel, move home, or strengthen your personal religious and spiritual beliefs.

This is a good location for an altar, shrine, or sacred space, if you have one in your home, or to display symbols or artwork relating to your spiritual beliefs.

Photographs of the people in your life who are particularly helpful also belong here, as do images or symbols that represent places you want to go or that have inspired you. Travel books belong here, as do white, gray, and black objects.

This is the section of the pa kua that will help you broaden your horizons in general, open your mind, and develop your lateral thinking skills. Use it if you feel stuck in a rut or want to bring some positive change into your life.

HOUSEHOLD GODS *This is a good area to situate any religious or spiritual symbols that you possess.*

AROUND THE WORLD *Cures placed in this area of the pa kua could have you traveling around the world. Be ready for positive change and adventure.*

51

focusing on...

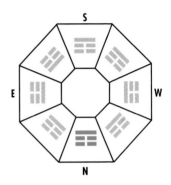

The Journey: Career. Our careers are important for our self-esteem and feelings of achievement. Use this section to enhance your career prospects and help you move on.

Journey of life

The Career section is also referred to as "The Journey" because it recognizes the fact that you go through different stages in your life and may try a range of jobs before you find the work that you love. Your progress toward meaningful and satisfying work is an important aspect of your life and does fit together seamlessly, no matter how many times you feel you are chopping and changing in your work. This is the area to enhance if you are

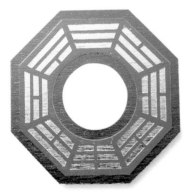

dissatisfied with your job, looking for new work or a change of direction, even if you don't know exactly what you want. Enhancements placed here will help to make the search for rewarding work flow more easily. They will also help you to clarify your ideas and work out what it is you want to do. Water features, mirrors, and artwork featuring water all make ideal cures, as does anything in dark colors,

WATER SYMBOL *Mirrors can be used to represent the water element. They also serve to reflect bad Chi away.*

LIFE FLOW *This section of the pa kua recognizes that our careers can take many twists and turns along the way.*

especially blue and black. If you choose to install a water feature, make sure the water stays fresh and clear—allowing it to stagnate is not advisable. Artwork showing water should also emphasize tranquil, deep flowing water. If you are already brooding on a lack of fulfillment in this area, pictures of dark or stormy waters—or desert scenes—will not fix the problem for you. Water is connected with this area because it represents the meandering river that changes direction but is always heading toward the same ultimate goal. Our lives progress in much the same way.

WATERY SCENES *Images depicting tranquil, gently moving water are a suitable cure for this area of the pa kua.*

53

focusing on...

Contemplation: Knowledge and Self-awareness. A key area for mental health and stability, use this pa kua section to enhance your inner poise and connection with yourself.

Inner peace

The trigram for this sector indicates "Mountain" and enhancements made here help to give you the time and space to be objective. When it is in balance, the energy from this sector helps you to cultivate serenity, to study more effectively, to make progress in personal development, and to meditate easily and fruitfully.

Appropriate cures include any books or materials associated with the subjects you are studying or want to know more about (this includes desks in students'

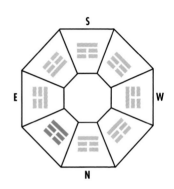

OFFICE FENG SHUI *You can easily enhance your work performance by moving your desk to a lucky position. Don't sit with your back to the door.*

BAD: BACK TO THE DOOR

GOOD: FACING THE DOOR

BAD: FACING THE DOOR DIRECT▮

DESK ENHANCERS

a bowl of fresh flowers

a small green plant

your telephone

your computer terminal

your cup of coffee

a light or something red

a lapis globe

a crystal paperweight

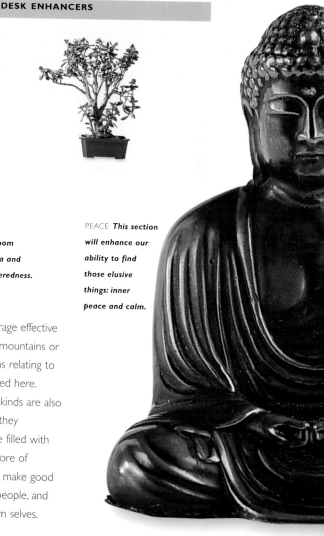

LIFE STUDY *Adding a desk your room enhances this section of the bagua and invites renewed serenity and centeredness. You can also use academic books.*

PEACE *This section will enhance our ability to find those elusive things: inner peace and calm.*

rooms if you want to encourage effective studying). Artwork featuring mountains or contemplative places, or items relating to meditation, are also well placed here. Containers and vessels of all kinds are also useful cures in this sector as they represent space waiting to be filled with knowledge or inspiration. A core of serenity and calm helps us to make good decisions, get on with other people, and also feel contented in our own selves.

55

focusing on...

Unity/Tao: The Center. At the heart of the pa kua lies the eternal meeting of Yin and Yang in dynamic harmony. This is a powerful area and should be kept clear.

Central calm

In the center of the pa kua we find the area referred to as Unity or Tao—where all things come together in balance and from where all energy emerges.

Historically many wealthy homes, not just in China and Asia, but elsewhere as well, have featured a central courtyard where plants or water features in particular encourage a gentle, revitalizing flow of energy and additional sunlight energizes all occupants.

As far as possible, keep this area clear of clutter in your home. Cures are also not very appropriate here as they can dramatically alter the effects of cures placed elsewhere in the home. Natural

PA KUA CENTER *The center of the pa kua is represented by the Yin Yang symbol. This circular device represents the energizing center of all things and the source of all harmony.*

crystals in particular are best avoided here. They become extremely powerful cures when placed at the center of the home and should be viewed as the last-ditch attempt to create change in your life. If you want change at any cost and intend to try this cure, put away all your other cures before you do so.

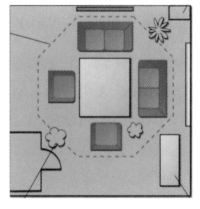

CALM IN THE MIDDLE **The best Feng Shui room layouts incorporate a central area of stillness, perhaps marked by a square or circular table.**

CRYSTALS OUT **Avoid using crystals, or any cure, in the central area of the home.**

MIDDLE WAY **Good floor plans have a central access area around which the rooms radiate.**

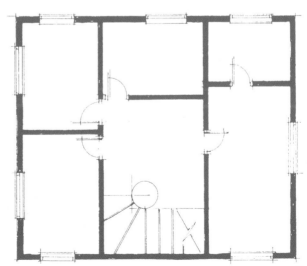

57

feng shui in the office

Whether your office is at home or in an open plan business space, there are some basic enhancements that can help to increase your effectiveness, prosperity, and success.

Desk magic

If you have a choice of desk shape and size, pick one that reflects the kind of work you need to do at it. Square or rectangular desks help to increase the flow of prosperity, while curved, oval, or round desks enhance creativity. A combination of curved and straight lines will help to improve both of these aspects whenever they are required in your work.

If you can't select a curved desk, but want to enhance creativity in your work, you can make adjustments by including space for plants on your desk. Plants are also extremely useful at absorbing the negative Chi emitted by computers and other electrical equipment.

LUCKY OFFICE **An auspicious office layout includes the desk positioned so that the door is easily visible.**

WEALTH CHARMS *Feng shui wealth charms will help to keep your business both productive and prosperous.*

You can place the pa kua on any flat surface, including your desk, in order to arrange things to your liking and to enhance your effectiveness at work.

If you have a choice of rooms for a home office, look at what you want to achieve before you choose. Auspicious pa kua possibilities include:

The Elders—this will bring more focus to your work and is especially useful if you want to be known as an authority in your field or to have others regarding you as a mentor.

Fortunate Blessings—the obvious solution, perhaps, if you are looking for steady growth and a minimum of problems with cash flow.

Fame and Reputation—this will help you to attract a lot of attention and acclaim for your work. This is particularly useful for those whose success depends on being in the public eye—journalists, authors, and marketing and public relations executives in particular.

ADDED CHARM *You can add lucky charms to office stationery such as accounts books to enhance wealth.*

Helpful Friends—if you want to inspire others, maintain respect, get help from a wider array of people, or if you are in the business of helping others (particularly good for teachers and agents). This will enhance communication skills.

feng shui in the yard

The yard can also benefit from the application of Feng Shui principles. You can use the pa kua in the same way as for rooms inside the home. Try to make sure that all the areas of the pa kua are represented.

Outer energy

Using Feng Shui in the yard can help to create a tranquil, lush, and inviting oasis. As with the home, you can place the pa kua on your yard, working with the colors, shapes, and habits of the plants to great effect. Take local conditions into account—so if the Fame area of your yard gets no sunlight, then your adjustments will need to involve plants with prickly or star-shaped leaves or red flowers (Fire element) or tall, upward-reaching plants (representing the Wood element).

Water features are of particular importance in the yard. The most auspicious arrangements will involve water flowing gently toward the house. If it flows away from the home, it will be draining

WATER MAGIC *Water features are key to the creation of a good Feng Shui yard. The sound of moving water also helps to enliven Chi and creates good luck.*

HANGING CHI *Hanging baskets of flower and lush plants are particularly good for enlivening Chi. Make sure that plants remain healthy and free of disease.*

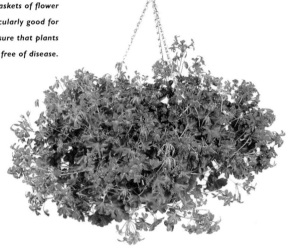

ou of energy and
pportunities to enhance
our prosperity.

Wildlife in the water,
articularly goldfish or koi,
lso help to keep it fresh and
revent stagnation. If you
an't bring in a water feature,

you can work with hanging baskets and trailing plants to suggest the appearance of flowing water instead. Don't forget to include a calm central area to relate to the center of the pa kua. This will generate Chi for the whole yard and help to keep plants healthy.

YARD CHARMS *There are plenty of symbols and charms that you can use in the garden. Decorative flowerpots will evoke the elements in color and design.*

index

acknowledgments

This is for my father, Terry Jenkins,

and for Judith Hale—friend and fellow enthusiast

Picture Credits: Liz Eddison Garden Photography 60l, Elizabeth Whiting Assoc's 32bl.